This book
belongs to

Murphy's Neighborhood Adventures

by

Martha Smith

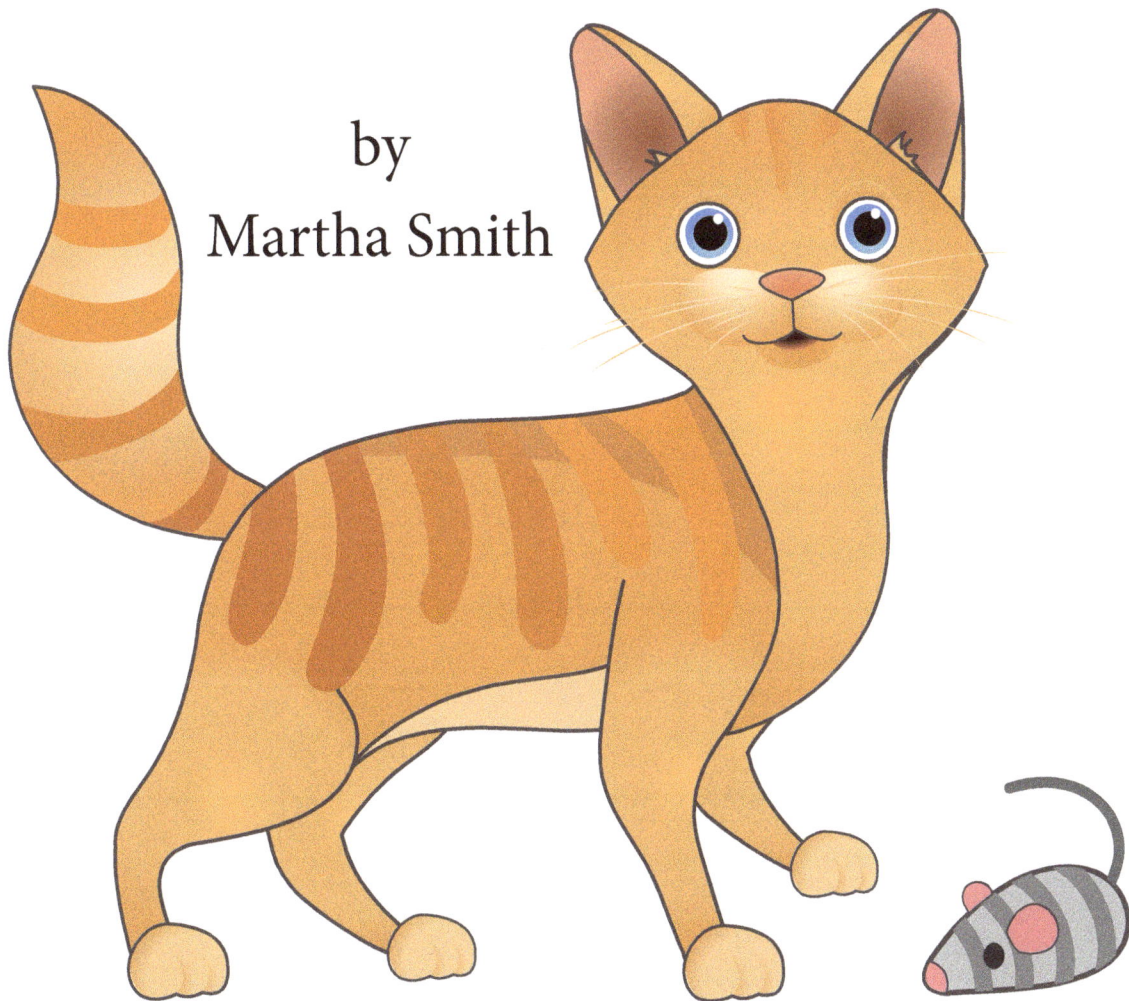

Illustrated by Jennifer Tipton Cappoen

Author: Martha Smith
Cover Designer and Illustrator: Jennifer Tipton Cappoen
Editor: Lynn Bemer Coble

PCKids is an imprint of **Paws and Claws Publishing, LLC.**
1589 Skeet Club Road, Suite 102 #175
High Point, NC 27265
www.PawsandClawsPublishing.com
info@pawsandclawspublishing.com

ISBN # 978-1-946198-29-7
Printed in the United States

Dedication

To my loving hubby, Danny,
for letting me read my story edits to you,
over and over and over again.

Murphy, the orange striped cat, was an extremely lucky cat. He knew it. He had been lucky two times already!

The first time when he felt lucky was when he was just a tiny kitten. He was adopted by a kind and friendly couple who lived on a quiet street in a small city.

At first he was an indoor cat and played all over the house. Murphy had comfy sofas and chairs to nap on, TVs to watch, and a huge bed to sleep on at night.

But Murphy became bored. The cat grew more and more curious about the world outdoors. He spent hours sitting and looking through the glass door.

One day, his mom watched him staring out the door. She wondered if Murphy wanted to go outdoors and explore.

When his mom held the door open for him, Murphy was surprised and a little scared of what was beyond. He decided to be brave and dashed out the door.

He was outside the house! No more boring days for Murphy. He had exciting new places to explore.

Murphy *loved* being outdoors! He prowled through the shrubs and grasses. He napped near the garden lined with round white stones.

He watched flittering butterflies, chased speedy lizards, and patted colorful flowers with his paws.

The cat especially liked lying under the shady, green shrubs. From there, he listened to the mishmash of sounds all around him in his neighborhood: chirping birds, croaking frogs, happy kids on bikes, noisy lawn mowers, and buzzing bees.

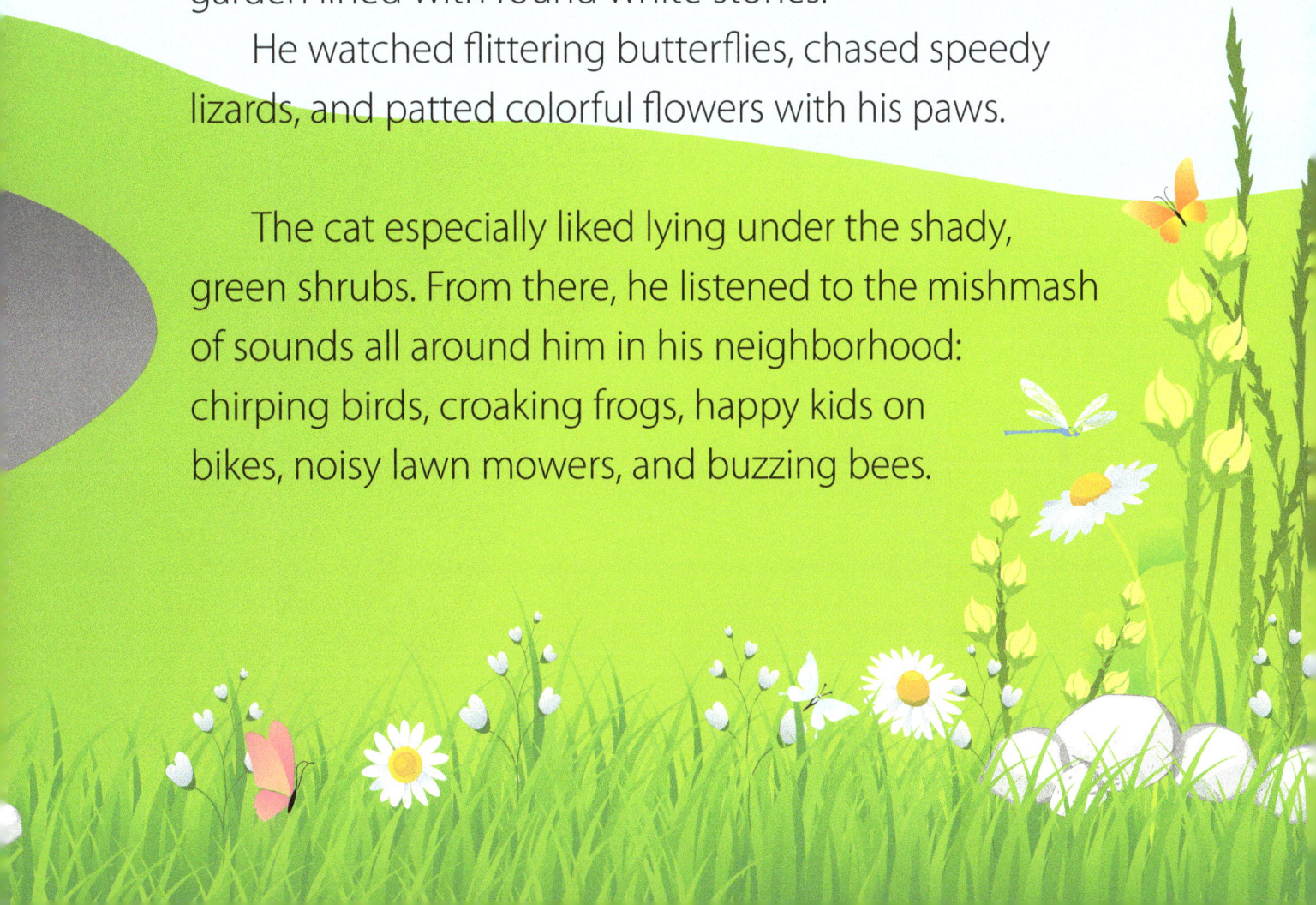

One day Murphy heard a sound. A *different* sound. He was instantly curious and decided to follow that sound. He walked a long way down the street and found Popsy working in his garage.

Murphy walked right into the garage. The cat looked around at all the strange and amazing things. Popsy quietly put down his tools and watched as Murphy explored the garage workshop.

Murphy thought this might be a fun place to hang out, so he did.

Each day Murphy slipped into the garage for a visit. Then the cat lay in the shade under Popsy's truck and watched as his friend repaired and cleaned things.

Popsy was a quiet man and Murphy liked watching him work. At times, Popsy looked over at Murphy and talked to him in a low, calm voice.

On each visit, Murphy strolled into the garage and rubbed his fur on Popsy's leg.

Later the cat just disappeared. Popsy was never sure where Murphy came from and where he went when he disappeared.

Sometimes when Popsy was drinking his morning coffee on the back deck, Murphy appeared, rubbed the man's leg, and disappeared toward the woods.

One morning while visiting Popsy, Murphy felt exceptionally brave. He let Popsy rub his head and back. Popsy rubbed Murphy's neck and played with his ears.

Then he paused and looked more closely at Murphy.

Murphy did *not* have a collar with tags around his neck.

Popsy sat and slowly drank his coffee. He thought and thought and thought about Murphy.

Where did Murphy live? Was Murphy a stray cat with no family of his own? Why did Murphy disappear into the woods after every visit? Where did he go?

It made Popsy feel unhappy to think that Murphy might be all alone with no one to care for him.

One day Popsy made a big decision. He decided to find out if Murphy had a family. His feline friend strolled into Popsy's garage as usual for his early-morning visit and head and back rub. The cat let Popsy rub his head and play with his ears just as he did most days.

While Popsy was rubbing the cat's ears, he lifted Murphy up and placed him in the front seat of the big red truck. Murphy wasn't scared of the truck at all. It was another place to explore!

Popsy started the truck. And down the steep driveway they went.

Murphy watched as the house got smaller and smaller as they drove down the street.

s Popsy drove the truck, the orange cat looked intently out the side window during their entire ride. *Oh my, all those things outside the truck window were amazing* thought Murphy. He stared at shiny cars, roaring motorcycles, strollers holding crying babies, laughing children, and yapping dogs.

One place they passed smelled so yummy that Murphy realized he was hungry. He certainly hoped that there was a special snack waiting for him when the truck ride was over.

WOOF!
WOOF!

DONATE
TO ANIMALS

VOLUNTEERS
NEEDED

ANIMAL
SHELTER

ADOPT
DON'T SHOP

They arrived at the local animal shelter. Popsy carried Murphy inside and walked straight to the front desk.

Murphy was instantly on alert. He heard the loud echoes of dogs barking, he smelled other cats nearby, and there were lots of strangers milling around. *Where were they? Why were they in this place? Why were all the animals in this building?* Oh, Murphy really hoped those noisy dogs would stay away from him.

The friendly woman at the check-in desk began rubbing Murphy's neck, his back, and his tummy. That back rub felt so soothing. Murphy just purred with pleasure.

Then the woman checked to see if the cat had a microchip that would allow her to find his family, their address, and their phone number in the computer.

Popsy waited while she checked Murphy for a chip. He felt happy and sad at the same time. If Murphy *didn't* have a chip, he was seriously thinking about making Murphy his new pet. If Murphy *did* have a chip, Popsy was going to be happy that Murphy would be going back to his real family. But if that happened, the man knew he would be a little let down to be losing his new friend.

The computer beeped. Yes, Murphy had a microchip. The helpful woman could see the name of the cat's family and their information on her screen.

Popsy smiled and thanked the woman for checking Murphy for the microchip and for finding Murphy's family's information. She told him that they would contact the cat's family and return Murphy to them.

BEEP!

Popsy gave Murphy one last big hug, rubbed his head one more time, and played with his ears.

Then he told his inquisitive cat friend good-bye, because Popsy knew that he might never see the cat again.

Murphy realized something important was happening. And the cat instinctively knew it didn't feel like a good thing. *Why in the world did his friend Popsy tell him good-bye? Didn't Popsy like him anymore? Had he done something that had made Popsy angry?*

ait! Wait! *Why was Popsy leaving him all alone in this strange place? In this place with the noisy barking dogs and all the strange people? Why was Popsy going away?* The two of them were supposed to get a snack after their trip in the big red truck. Then they were supposed to drive back to Popsy's garage. *Had Popsy forgotten?*

Murphy was confused. The cat was more than a little scared.

Popsy drove his big red truck back home. He already missed seeing Murphy on the front seat beside him. He was feeling a little blue because he'd grown so accustomed to the daily visits from his little orange friend.

Early the next day, Popsy brewed his coffee. He carried his steaming mug out to the back deck as he did every morning.

He sat there, thought about Murphy, and puzzled over where the cat really lived. Popsy wondered if Murphy's family members were excited to get him back.

All of a sudden, Popsy heard a faint meow from nearby. He looked around. There was *Murphy* sitting on the steps looking down at him.

Murphy strolled over—the same way he usually did—to get his neck and back rubbed. He wanted Popsy to play with his ears. Then the orange cat settled down beside Popsy's feet for a little nap.

Popsy was pretty sure Murphy was smiling as he slept.

Later that morning, a woman arrived looking for Murphy. She saw Popsy and Murphy working together in the garage. She told the man her name. Then she explained that Murphy lived just down the street and wasn't really lost at all.

Popsy was delighted to hear that and asked her if Murphy could keep visiting him.

Murphy heard what his friend said and gave an unusually boisterous cat purr.

This was the second time the orange cat felt lucky.

Murphy was going to be able to keep visiting his new friend Popsy. He could see a bright future that included soothing back and neck rubs, long naps in the shade, and special times spent working with Popsy in his garage.

THE END

About the Author

Martha Smith grew up near the small town of Dublin, Georgia. She and her husband currently reside in Martinsville, Virginia. She owns Smith River Vintage, an online source for all things vintage, antique, or unique.

Martha loves reading, bike riding, camping, and flea markets. She is an avid knitter and enjoys making and donating hats to nearby cancer-treatment centers.

Martha writes animal-themed children's books with a mixture of nonfiction and fiction. Throughout her years of traveling, Martha has witnessed many amusing animal antics. Those stories are just waiting to be told, …so stay tuned.

www.ingramcontent.com/pod-product-compliance
Lightning Source LLC
LaVergne TN
LVHW070841080426
835513LV00024B/2429